THE WIT
OF
BRENDAN
BEHAN

THE WIT
OF
BRENDAN
BEHAN

Compiled by Sean McCann

LESLIE FREWIN : LONDON

First published 1968 by
Leslie Frewin Publishers Limited,
One New Quebec Street, Marble Arch, London W1

Second Impression 1970

This book is set in 12 on 14 point Bembo,
printed by Anchor Press and bound by
Wm Brendon, both of Tiptree, Essex

World Rights Reserved

09 090060 X

Contents

Introduction

'NO MAN SHOULD be without a BB in his life,' roared Brendan
Behan across a Dublin stage one night when the Brigitte
Bardot image was young. 'Maybe I haven't the same figure
or the same face or even the same sort of talent but we're
both in the same business. She's an entertainer and so am I.'

The same Brendan entertained with words . . . the sort
of words that always kept his audience hungry . . . and kept
them wondering just what would come next. 'He wrote,'
said the poet Louis MacNeice, 'with plenty of hyperbole
and emphasis. He was a man of humanity, gusto and formidable wit.' Formidable indeed. His totally disordered life
consumed a measure of porter that should not obscure the
fact that he was one of the great Irish wits – comparable
indeed with Wilde or Shaw. He was also flamboyant and
rambunctious . . . and inevitable.

Everything he wrote was Himself. He wrote it from the
heart of the turnip-like figure with the bird-spurting walk;
from inside the open square yard or so of hairy chest that
perpetually thrust itself through an unbuttoned shirt.

Brendan Behan was the talker talking. The writing was

just a way of letting the world know what he was saying. There was hardly a story he told that he didn't write and there was hardly a quip he wrote that he didn't repeat and repeat, again and again. 'I'm like Shaw,' he once said, 'I always quote myself – it adds spice to the conversation.' Spice indeed and emphasis. He always knew the value of a good story and wasn't afraid to twist the facts to fit the moment. That's why in Dublin today there are so many different versions of the same story . . . only different, if you know what I mean.

This collection of stories has been gathered from very many sources and it shows only one side of Brendan . . . the witty talker and writer. But add to this a vaudevillian sense of comedy; the versatility of the true ego pricker; the happy boyish belief that you can find a good man anywhere; and then, for perversity's sake, throw in the drinker, the fighter, the rebel, the borstal boy, the 'pudding cheenis' and you have the complex figure that was Brendan Behan. Yet behind all these was another side . . . the serious writer; the man who was conscious that he had a contribution to make to world writing and who critics believe made it with his magnificent *Borstal Boy*.

The entertainer in Brendan was bred in him – in the Queen's Theatre, where one branch of the family, the Bourkes, had a stake. Brendan was there often as a youngster and never forgot the simple lessons of the variety theatre that in later years had him busking outside London's theatres or entertaining the assembled company in a Dublin pub or raising roofs in Greenwich Village.

He had his wits about him from the cradle, and his mother, Kathleen, remembers many of his childish pranks: 'I remember once – he was only about five – when he toddled out and into a neighbour's house where the family was having breakfast. The woman had just put on some eggs to boil when she saw the extra visitor coming in. Being poor she couldn't afford an egg for little Brendan but she put a cup of tea and some buttered bread in front of him. Brendan looked mournfully at the plate and when the woman asked him if he had lost his appetite he turned to the boy sitting beside him and said: "Hello, egg." '

If you take this as the beginning of the stories of the wit of Brendan Behan the compiler knows he has a long road to travel and unravel. The yarns trip in easily. Stories of his great antics with the poet Patrick Kavanagh – how he painted the Kavanagh flat when the poet was on holidays, for free. But for devilment he painted it a total black. How in a famous court case when a witness denied three times that he knew Behan there came a 'cock-a-doodle-doo' from the back of the courthouse. How he set up office in the burnt-out shell of the old Abbey Theatre and put a notice over the door 'The town office of Brendan Francis Behan'. He used it for months before the managing director, Ernest Blythe, found him out.

Possibly it was in this 'town office' that the writing really took shape. It seems likely it was here the first really witty writings found their creation before being despatched to the newsroom of the *Irish Press* on the opposite side of the Liffey. These Behan columns began in 1954 (some of them have since been collected under the general title of *Hold Your Hour and Have Another*) and they ring of the true Behan and the real Dublin.

Snatches from the streets of Dublin, from the old lags in prison, from the bookies' runners, from the painters and decorators . . . Behan carried them all into his conversation and into his books. His spirit was such that he was the most entertaining man of Liffeyside for many a year. Even in his last days the spark would still flicker as when a friend said to him: 'I thought you were in hospital.' Then opening his almost toothless mouth he grinned: 'I was – but I escaped.'

Today wherever you go in Dublin you will hear the stories of the wit of Brendan Behan. I hope I have caught the essence of it in this book . . . and if you happen to know a Behan story that is not included I would like to hear it, they all deserve cataloguing. To the many people who helped me with tape recordings, cuttings and even diaries I am extremely grateful. To Brendan's wife, Beatrice, who has always been so helpful and courteous; to his mother, Kathleen, and her late husband, Stephen; to publicans, especially Michael O'Connoll at the 'White Horse'; to theatre producers, actors, to editors and reporters and art editors, especially the *Irish Press*, who gave me permission to quote from the many articles Brendan wrote. There are so many others – librarians, Miss Mairin O'Byrne, Benedict Kiely, Kevin Sullivan, John B. Keane, Anthony Butler, and researchers in New York, London, Paris and Toronto. To everyone my grateful thanks.

SEAN McCANN

THE WIT
OF
BRENDAN
BEHAN

Behanism

'*The writer in Brendan was continually in danger of being shouted down by the talker, the playwright upstaged by the vaudevillian, the artist elbowed aside by the anecdotist,*' wrote Kevin Sullivan, *but all the time Brendan had his tricks and his improvisations completely under control. He had something to say about everything – no matter if it was the daily wit of the Dubliner assuring someone who had done him a good turn:* '*Your blood's worth bottlin*',' *no matter if it was the remaking of a Shaw or Wilde saying: coming from Brendan it assumed a new class title –* '*A Behanism*'.

*   *   *

The most important thing to do in this world is to get something to eat, something to drink and somebody to love you.

*   *   *

To many people ambition is a way of working themselves to death to live better.

*   *   *

If you are in good health, and have the price of a drink, death and love can be mourned in comfort.

*   *   *

If you don't get up and get down town you'd hear nothing, nor find out what they're saying about you. And in the name of God, they're saying something. Good or bad, it's better to be criticised than ignored.

*   *   *

Praise:

May your shadow never grow less.

*   *   *

If it's a thing I go in for in a human being, it's weakness. I'm a devil for it.

*   *   *

Hunger makes pornographers of us all.

*   *   *

I have a total irreverence for anything connected with society except that which makes the roads safer, the beer stronger, the food cheaper, the old men and old women warmer in the winter and happier in the summer.

* * *

Success is damn near killing me. If I had my way, I should prescribe that success should go to every man for a month; then he should be given a pension and forgotten.

* * *

It's nobody's fault to be a bastard but to be a dastard you have to work at it.

* * *

He'd drink porter out of a polisman's boots.

* * *

Gimme a pint of stout and a bottle be the neck.

* * *

Dates are only for the police.

* * *

The bloody car we went in was only held together by St Christopher medals.

*　　*　　*

The principal aim in this world after the age of sixteen should be comfort.

*　　*　　*

The wicked prosper in a wicked world.

*　　*　　*

In matters of sentiment there can be nothing but non-sensicality.

*　　*　　*

It's a queer world, but the best we've got to be going on with.

*　　*　　*

Every tinker has his way of dancing and every cripple his way of walking.

*　　*　　*

In a new town the first thing a tinker looks at is his horse.

*   *   *

A city is a place where you were least likely to get a bite of a wild sheep.

*   *   *

There's many a man that's cursed with the body of Charles Atlas – in reverse.

*   *   *

A job is death without the dignity.

*   *   *

Travel is a great inducer of gloom.

*   *   *

We keep the past for pride.

*   *   *

How's the form? is a frequent Dublin question that has an inevitable follow-up – one that Brendan always used.

Very good. As a matter of fact, if I was better I couldn't stick it.

* * *

Nobody should be impressed with the Sputnik or the Bluenick or any other nick.

* * *

The Arctic – or better still the Antarctic – should be declared the World's battleground and any war not taking place there should immediately be proclaimed illegal.

* * *

The suffering from the H-bomb won't last as long as the suffering during the Depression.

* * *

The world is sometimes a tough place but you were never in a worse position to meet cruelty than as a schoolboy.

* * *

On the Blue Train you can look in the windows of the Pullman and see the rich settling down for a banquet of some hundreds of miles, and I've no doubt you could order anything from a live trout to a young child, if you fancied it and had the money to pay for it, or the money to go first class.

* * *

The only people I ever met who really believed in capital punishment were murderers.

* * *

Go on, ye bowsie, your blood's in your knuckles.

* * *

Nearly all thieves are Tories.

* * *

Tradition is the most persistent of man's creations.

* * *

He once described the voice of a woman singer as resembling:

The throttling of cats . . . one verse from her would clear a parish.

* * *

Have you ever seen the chorus girls in the Queen's Theatre? They call them the Moonbeams; they're a group of well-ventilated lovelies.

*   *   *

God be with the youth of us and the simple pleasures of the poor.

*   *   *

What can't be cured must be endured.

*   *   *

You can't blame George Kleinsinger's mynah bird for committing homicide. There are very few people of my generation all over the world who haven't been just as savage.

*   *   *

Killing your wife is a natural class of a thing could happen to the best of us.

*   *   *

Sometimes he would quote from prison jargon:

Do you mean we're getting food with our meals today?

*   *   *

Corkmen and Northerners are the hardest to hang . . . they've such bloody hard necks.

*　　　*　　　*

There are some that did me as many good turns as a corkscrew.

*　　　*　　　*

With the winter over and Christmas past you wouldn't feel a day over ninety.

*　　　*　　　*

Jews have necks as hard as a jockey's rump.

*　　　*　　　*

If an ass is born in a stable, does that make it a horse?

*　　　*　　　*

One might be out of the world as out of the fashion.

*　　　*　　　*

God gives us the brains; it's no credit to ourselves.

*　　　*　　　*

Anybody would think you was doing God a good turn speaking well of him.

*   *   *

The way some civil servants talk you'd think God was in another department.

*   *   *

My favourite brand of civil servants are the diplomats. From Lyons to Lewis I have found them a help and protection to the wandering Irish taxpayer, and altogether very good value.

*   *   *

A shut mouth catches no flies.

*   *   *

What was right yesterday can well be wrong tomorrow . . . and vice versa.

*   *   *

Ireland is a figment of Anglo-Saxon imagination.

*   *   *

Country people are as talkative as the tomb.

Himself – by Himself

Large of heart, loose of tongue, sometimes as loveable as a panda, sometimes obscene, rumbustious, bawdy, a thesaurus with a Rabelaisian flavour . . . you find the word or the phrase and it fits Brendan.

He saw himself a nurse, an ordinary person, a pet, a Caucasian, a strict Dubliner – even as a stroke of 'bloody good luck'. Certainly he was never short of a description of himself or of his role in life.

*　　*　　*

In a now famous interview with Eamonn Andrews he said:

I'm a very ordinary person. A great number of people say that with their tongue in their cheek, but I say it with my tongue in my gums! I've a great deal of fame, a certain amount of glory, a certain amount of infamy. And I can only repeat, with John Keat's saying: 'God help the poor little famous.'

*　　*　　*

His interview for the film The Quare Fellow *was probably the most probing one that Brendan ever allowed. Asked by Eamonn Andrews how he saw himself in the world he said:*

Whistler, the English painter, remarked that the world is divided into two classes: invalids and nurses. I'm a nurse. I try to show the world to a certain extent what's the matter with it.

* * *

Brendan held court during the mid fifties in the 'White Horse', next door to the Irish Press. *Often he told his audience:*

The world is made up of four sexes – men, women, old men and old women – and I have never in my travels met anything worse than myself.

* * *

God forgive us – but most of us grew up to be the sort of men our mothers warned us against.

* * *

As a child I was a 'bit of a hard chaw'. The mother said there was so much divilment in me that I would hang a parish. The father said he didn't know where he got me – and me only a high infant in William Street!

* * *

I was reared a pet, God help me.

* * *

He was educated by the Christian Brothers:

It was a day of rejoicing the day I left school; that was the day the Brothers realised that if you pray long enough your every wish will be God's desire.

* * *

Referring to his education one day when someone on the Irish Press *asked him if he had read a certain book:*

I need sympathy. I only went to school half time – when they were teaching the writing. I missed the reading.

* * *

I was reared a strict Dubliner. My father's people came from the cul-de-sac (not a French word by the way, they call it 'impasse') called 'George's Pocket' at the back of St George's Church in Temple Street, which is the most beautiful bit of city anywhere.

* * *

We lived in a tenement – and since our own took over they've gone through the slums like the wrath of God.

* * *

Nostalgia for Georgian Dublin is all right when you don't happen to have lived in one of those relics of a King of England.

* * *

I am, as the poet said, tulip shaped and anyone that has seen me sideways on knows that I'm not a square.

* * *

More specifically he once said to Tim Pat Coogan:

If I had my lips rouged and my tits pushed out I'd be a ringer for Lilian Roth.

* * *

Once in his more rotund days, novelist Francis MacManus saw him pretending to buss a very stout, good-humoured lady. Their equators prevented conjunction. Shouted Behan:

The spirit is willing but the flesh is in the way.

* * *

On a question of colour he said he recognised no colour bar.

To be more to the point I only recognise one bar –

Michael O'Connell's at St George's Quay. As for white skins, the only really white man I've seen was a dead one.

*　　*　　*

I'm a Caucasian according to American standards; a European by promotion; and an Irishman by a stroke of bloody good luck.

*　　*　　*

His first job was at house painting. He said that he was like another tradesman in the same line and could agree that:

Putty and paint made the carpenter a saint.

*　　*　　*

House painting is a bloody dirty and dangerous job.

*　　*　　*

I wasn't without ambition in the painting, graining, marbling and lettering game but it was generally accepted that my real talents lay in the placing of bookie's dockets.

*　　*　　*

I was allergic to painting – and if you had an air you could make a song of that.

*　　*　　*

27

The only person I ever knew in Ireland to refuse honest employment at trade union rates is myself.

*   *   *

Once, in a pub that was being decorated, Brendan was asked to lend a hand.

Good luck but I'm allergic to paint brushes and afraid of knives. Putty knives, hacking knives and glazing knives.

*   *   *

I'd paint a ceiling for Royalty as long as they paid the going rate.

*   *   *

Brendan told how he once lost a house-painting job:

It was a morning after and I fell asleep. Like a child. Until I heard a door opening. Cute as a Christian I didn't move but I heard the foreman say: 'Sleep on, Behan, sleep on, for while ye're asleep ye have a job but as soon as ye wake ye're sacked.' It was the most comfortable sleep I ever had – knowing I was being paid for it.

*   *   *

His great love was a swim – in Tara Street baths or at the many bathing places around Dublin. He expressed it easily:

I love the sea – but a day in the country is a bloody long time.

*   *   *

He wasn't always worried about the convention of dressing when swimming. Once on a crowded beach he ran to the water with not a stitch on, roaring as he went:

Close your eyes, girls, I'm coming through.

*   *   *

Somebody on a crowded beach once remarked that he had no clothing on when he got out of the water and he said:

No, but I don't mind; for one half of you is men and the other is actresses.

*   *   *

Brendan liked to go to the greyhound races and in a moment of despair after backing a row of losers said:

The man who said that the more he saw of mankind the more he liked his dog was some sort of informer, a man that his own mother would run away from, if she could only lose him in a big enough crowd.

*   *   *

A landlady once asked him what he did for a living.

I thought of saying I was a progress-chaser or a Power Samas operator, but for both these occupations you have to have false teeth and a taste for sausage rolls, so I said I was interested in cattle.

*   *   *

Brendan met a man on the plane to New York who was reluctant to say exactly what he did for a living.

No harm to you. I'm rather reluctant to say what I do.

*   *   *

I have a sense of humour that would nearly cause me to laugh at a funeral, providing it wasn't my own.

*   *   *

Politically, Brendan said he wasn't a Communist.

I'm too humble and modest. The Communists want to

free all the workers of the world. I'm content to make a start and free one member of it at a time – myself.

*   *   *

He once told a colleague whose book had been slated:

You're too thin-skinned. Sure if I took notice of my critics, I'd been in the mad house long ago.

*   *   *

After a hospital stay he came out smiling and happy. Greeted by the world's press he announced:

The doctors tell me that I have a liver like a hobnailed boot.

*   *   *

To a visiting writer who described Brendan as a writer and folk singer:

Folk singers I detest; I would shoot every one of them. They get an old banjo in their hands and they call themselves folk singers. Now my uncle wrote Irish songs, and I also learnt songs off my mother, who has never stopped singing. Not even the Depression could stop her. I can sing in Irish and English and I've had an odd stab at singing in French, but I never knew I was a folk singer.

*   *   *

Never afraid to sing a song he boasted that the best money he ever got for this side of his talents was:

Twenty thousand francs from Radio Diffusion Française – at 2 o'clock in the morning.

*   *   *

After appearing on Michael O hAodha's Radio Eireann programme:

Singing seems to be an easy way of lining a coffin.

*   *   *

Once singing a popular song in Boland's pub in Stillorgan:

Farewell to cold winter,
Spring has come at last,
Nothing have I gained
But my true love I have lost. . . .

As regards that last part of the transaction it's a question of who's losing who!

*   *   *

Lady Chatterley's Lover had a certain fascination for Brendan. He had his own version of the song – and sang it often. The opening verse went:

(Ca

An unusually quiet moment captured by the camera of
Lord Snowdon.

Temporarily teetotal!

I'm Lady Chatterley's Lover,
A game gamekeeper that's me,
I love my pheasant and plover
But mostly I love Lady C.

*　　　*　　　*

Coming back from one of his many French visits he was accosted by a journalist in the 'White Horse' as he started to write his weekly Irish Press *column. 'Have you got* Lady Chatterley's Lover?' *he was asked.*

What the hell do you think? If I had it I wouldn't be wasting my time writing books. I'd be selling it!

*　　　*　　　*

I'm a mirror. I mirror what happens to people, the ordinary people. And the ordinariness of people is what is often extraordinary.

*　　　*　　　*

This is the truth – I'm a neurotic. My neuroses are the nails and harness which give me a living. If they cured me I'd have to go back to house-painting.

*　　　*　　　*

His bad language worried him sometimes:

I know it's bad but how the effin' hell can I write the way Irishmen talk if I don't use the effin' word. After all that effer Lawrence got away with it. It's a word that's part of our international heritage.

* * *

His extreme vulgarity was often aroused by gentility. Seated one snowy, cold day on the sea wall of the Liffey he saw passing on the other side of the broad quay a well-known nature writer. He roared at her like an articulate polar bear:

Hey, missus, how's the blue tits?

* * *

Frequently he resorted to the Irish language to talk with friends. One night he was speaking Gaelic in a London pub when a London porter said to him: 'Speak English and stop making a show of yourself.' Said Brendan afterwards:

You can judge for yourself the reply he got from me in the mellifluous tongue of Shakespeare, Milton and Johnson.

* * *

Once asked by a reporter if he was married and if he had any family, he replied:

I'm married to Beatrice Salkeld, a painter – that's an artist-painter. By nature she's a happier and far more amiable sort of person, She has to be. We have no children at the moment – except me.

*　　*　　*

It has never been a habit of mine to say anything bad about meself.

*　　*　　*

After his marriage to Beatrice Salkeld ('my first wife') he lived in a couple of houses before moving to the Embassy-covered district of Ballsbridge, the most exclusive suburb in Dublin. There Beatrice and he took up residence behind a dull red door with no bell or knocker and the word 'Cuig' (Irish for five) on the gate. Brendan growled at me once:

How did I get here? I paid for the effin' place to give it a tone of respectability.

*　　*　　*

Eamonn Andrews: What would you like to have said to you in fifty years' time?
Brendan: That I've celebrated my eighty-sixth, my eighty-seventh birthday!

Da, Ma and Others

The name Behan will long be remembered in Dublin. The family burst out in a flower of genius in the 1950s. Stories that once were family tales became national jokes. 'I remember Brendan fell into the canal. Drownin' he was . . . and I ran into the Behans . . . and what d'yeh think they said? . . . What d'yeh think? "Is that so?" cum the answer, "Is that so? Ah, sure the Lord looks after his own", and nara move they made.' Grannies, uncles, father and mother provided, through Brendan, an extra dimension to the wit of the Irish.

*   *   *

My Granny's favourite toast was: 'Here's to the harp of old Ireland, and may it never want for a string as long as there's a gut in the peeler', and I am not that mad about police of any sort myself.

*   *   *

'Do you know the difference between having an Irish

Republic and being a section of the British Empire?' my granny often asked me.

No, says I, what is it?

'From one you'll get an eviction order written in English with the lion and the unicorn, and from the other an eviction order written in Irish with a harp.'

* * *

My grandfather was a moderate man who believed in having a pint and a half one, every ten minutes but not making a beast of himself.

* * *

My grand aunt died in a state of acute indignation brought on by someone letting her hear Churchill's speech at the end of the war.

* * *

One day in a butcher's shop looking at a sheep's head the granny asked me if I ever thought sheep could look so vindictive. 'It's more like the head of my old man,' she said, blessing herself.

* * *

My uncle Peader Kearney, who wrote the Irish National Anthem, was a sort of walking battery of Fenianism.

*　　*　　*

An aunt of mine went to the GPO on Easter Monday 1916 when the fighting was going on. She refused to get away and kept demanding to see her husband. He finally came to a sandbagged window and roared: 'Go away, Maggie,' and she shouted back: 'I only wanted to know if you were going to your work in the morning.'

*　　*　　*

Another aunt lived along the banks of the Canal:

She always was invitin' us to drop in whenever we passed.

*　　*　　*

My family have always had an interest – let me say a proprietary interest – in the Royal Canal . . . so much so that the great aunt gave us permission to swim in it.

*　　*　　*

The Da once told me there were three places to keep out of when I grew up – the country, the Continent, and the benighted bloody city of Belfast.

*　　*　　*

My mother once said: 'Anything that shocks Brendan Behan would turn thousands grey.'

*   *   *

My father's favourite story – well, one of them anyway – is of the raffle which had as a first prize a week in Belfast and the second prize a fortnight.

*   *   *

Explaining his parents' absence from town:

My father and mother are off to London to assist in the inauguration of a new niece.

*   *   *

Whenever anyone asked his father, Stephen, why he wasn't a writer or a playwright himself he replied:

I've been too bloody busy producing the writers.

*   *   *

Like Sean O'Casey, the greatest playwright living in my opinion, my family's land was all in window-boxes. Then in the swift switch of humour he would admit that digging was an activity he wouldn't pick for pleasure and would tell how his father, Stephen, during a Dublin strike brought him out to help farm an eighth of an acre of land at Glasnevin, once associated with Dean Swift. Stephen dug for a bit with great function, talked about the land, how his ancestors came from it, how healthy it was, and how if they kept at the digging they might uncover relics of Swift or Vanessa or Stella or Mrs Delaney. But next day, bored, he got a countryman to dig the plot in exchange for Stephen doing the countryman's strike picket duty.

*　　　*　　　*

Miss McCann, who worked a sewing-machine, making habits for the dead, lived near the Behan family.

She did a steady line and she didn't have to be always buying patterns, for the fashions didn't change, not even from summer to winter.

*　　　*　　　*

There was this oul' lady of some seventy summers lived near us, which if you count the winters too would leave her about a hundred and forty, and she looked it and not a day more.

*　　　*　　　*

Round our way there were many candidates for the brain

garage. They were victims of the Great War, the Black and Tan War, the Civil War, and the Economic War, when we were all a bit hatcha from eating free beef.

*   *   *

When we got our notice to move from Russell Street one oul' one moaned to my mother about cannibalism in Kimmage four miles away. 'Oh! Mrs Behan, don't go out to Kimmage – that's where they ate their young.'

*   *   *

Stephen Behan was being complimented on the success of his sons after appearing on This is Your Life. '*I see Brendan is doing well,*' *said the man.*

Indeed he is. Last year he wore my cast-offs now I'm wearing his.

*   *   *

The opinion of a wife is no certificate of worthiness, less than a parents', for a wife does more than love the wayward child, she takes over the matured and finished sinner.

As He Saw Others

Brendan lived a life of chronic restlessness – a restlessness that brought him into contact with people in every walk of life. He liked talking about the people he met and was never more pleased than when he was invited to President Kennedy's inauguration. He liked talking about his conversations with Elizabeth Taylor – 'For a few minutes you'd think we were hypochondriacs,' he'd say laughing. Another occasion: ' "Muggeridge," I said to Malcolm, "that's a name that starts you off at a disadvantage right away." ' Gilbert Harding, Oona Guinness, John Betjeman and Hemingway were just a few of his friends. Often he had a personal contact with people too long dead for him to have known – 'as my mother said to Yeats . . .', 'I delivered milk to Joyce's sister . . .' – but there was always an element of fun and surprise in his stories.

*　　　*　　　*

Allen Ginsberg introduced me to another poet who gets a hundred dollars a month from Uncle Sam for being mad. In Ireland, a poet has to do it for nothing.

*　　　*　　　*

Norman Mailer gave a party in Brooklyn . . . I could nearly tell you all about it – I say nearly because it was a bloody good party.

*　　*　　*

About Ernest Hemingway and Liam O'Flaherty:

There's plenty of violence in my writings but I am not so childishly pleased about it as they are.

*　　*　　*

Samuel Beckett is an old and good friend of mine, he's also a marvellous playwright. I don't know what his plays are about, but I enjoy them. I don't know what a swim in the sea is, but I enjoy it. I enjoy the water flowing over me.

*　　*　　*

For me to praise Shaw or O'Casey would be a piece of impertinence. It would be like praising the lakes of Killarney . . . saying they were rather nice looking.

*　　*　　*

My mother was a maid in a house where Yeats came to lunch. He would eat anything and half the time he didn't even know what he was eating. He'd put sugar in the soup and salt in the coffee and the only bloody thing he'd turn up his nose at was parsnips. Once the mother served parsnips to him by mistake and he sniffed and said: 'This is a very peculiar pudding.'

*   *   *

A well-known Evening Herald *columnist was talking quietly to a friend in Dublin's fashionable Grafton Street one day when hailed by Brendan from the other sidewalk.*

How's the writing going? That oul' column of yours is only retail business. Why don't you get into the wholesale trade like me? Books . . . plays . . . money.

*   *   *

One night Thornton Wilder, who was with James Thurber, asked me why I didn't stay in the United States. I told him that Dublin was my home. He said: 'They'll only give you what they gave all their other great literary men eventually – abuse.' I said that the Irish people eventually voted with their feet at the box office.

*   *   *

Mr Robert Morley has the indifference to criticism that comes of success.

*   *   *

There's some bloody blokes I know who would never be satisfied – even with a suite in the Ritz and Rita Hayworth.

* * *

Lenin and meself are in the same camp in one way – we believe that the main object of politics should be the abolition of the village idiot.

* * *

Shakespeare said pretty well everything, and what he left out, James Joyce, with a nudge from meself, put in.

* * *

Myself and Winston – that's Churchill to you – have at least one thing in common . . . we were once members of the same organisation. He was an elder brother of Trinity House and I was a painter for Irish Lights. I ought to add that his position was more decorative than functional.

* * *

Every officer in the Irish Army is a general – like their mothers before them.

* * *

Brendan once wrote in The People:

Fred Boland's wife, who outrivals Tallulah Bankhead for wit, is an old associate of mine. We painted the Four Provinces ballroom together. Mrs Boland (Frances Kelly, the artist) painted the pictures and I painted walls.

She is famous for her remark to a London shop assistant. Mrs Boland told the girl to send her purchases to the Irish Embassy.

'Irish Embassy?' said the girl. 'I thought you were in our Empire.'

'Didn't know you had one,' replied the elegant Ambassadress.

As Others Saw Him

Wherever Brendan went instant recognition went too. Fame was always at his side but now and again she changed costumes with notoriety. And this left Brendan open to the comments of the world. And everyone had their words to offer – commentators, critics, judges, police, organisers, barmen . . . Brendan Behan was just something you could not miss.

* * *

Ed Murrow, after he had cut Behan out of a Small World *discussion:*

We have encountered difficulties beyond our control.

Jackie Gleeson, who was in the same show:

Brendan came over 100 proof. It wasn't an Act of God but an act of Guinness.

New York's Daily News *on the same show:*

If the celebrated playwright wasn't pickled he gave the best imitation of rambling alcoholism you ever saw.

Columbia Broadcasting System's explanation:

Behan started sober as a judge – what happened afterwards was unexpected – and unavoidable. During delays in shooting Behan excused himself frequently and made trips to another room. His condition became progressively worse each time he returned.

*   *   *

Says Benedict Kiely:

He was the most entertaining companion I've ever known. One night in Michael O'Connell's 'White Horse' he had us sick with laughter at his antics. One minute he was Toulouse-Lautrec, walking up and down the floor on his knees; the next he was The Poor Old Woman, Mother Ireland, with the tail of his coat over his head for a shawl; then an aspiring Irish politician mouthing every platitude ever heard from an Irish platform and borrowing a few from the pulpit; and then sex in the Abbey Theatre, for which there were no words but only a very personal mime. I remember thinking then if he only got a wider audience he'd make a fortune.

*   *   *

Laid low with an infected arm, Brendan rests in preparation
for his visit to New York for the Broadway production of
The Hostage.

(Radio Times Hulton Picture Library)

In the Fitzroy Tavern in 1956.

With his wife Beatrice.

(Camera Press)

Another of Benedict Kiely's favourite stories of Brendan concerns the time when the Behan name was better known for house painting than for writing.

Brendan painted the flat of the poet, Patrick Kavanagh, for free but, for laughs, did it, in the poet's absence, a complete and total sable.

*　　*　　*

On a couple of occasions when his play The Hostage *was being played in London's Wyndham Theatre, Brendan burst in rumpled and crumpled and panicked the cast. Among the audience on the first occasion was playwright R F Delderfield, who described the scene:*

Phil the Fluther's Ball looked like an English Sunday-school party compared with the show. Brendan's main line of attack was against the cast. 'Why don't you do the play properly?' he shouted. 'Why don't you shut up?' called back the cast. After that there was no holding Brendan. He shouted the lines just before the actors and then sang a ballad. An anguished manager appealed to the audience: 'How can I throw him out? He's the author.'

*　　*　　*

The Irish Times *in its portrait gallery summed up the Behan situation:*

There are persons of bourgeois respectability in the city of Dublin who nourish a secret unease. It is that one day they may be proceeding on their middle-class way, chatting smoothly with their employer or their bank manager, when suddenly across the street will come a loud and ebullient 'View-halloo' followed by a colourful and uninhibited commentary on things in general. It will, of course, be Mr Brendan Behan, who enjoys carrying on conversations with the width of the street between himself and his interlocuter. Mr Behan has the voice for it but few of his friends have the nerve. Still, it is one of the occupational risks involved in knowing Mr Behan, and all who know him have decided that it is worth it.

*   *   *

Banning him from New York's St Patrick's Day Parade, Justice James J Comerford said:

By his reputation in the press here and abroad he is a disorderly person, so let him stay on the stage where he belongs.

*   *   *

After being arrested in McGoo's beer parlour in Hollywood Brendan was bailed out by manager Jerry Brentori, who had previously had him arrested.

I telephoned Brendan when they refused to let him in the St Patrick's Day Parade in New York. I asked him to come out here and celebrate with us. Tonight he showed up and I wish he hadn't.

*   *   *

Irish Press *reporter:*

There is no doubt that the secret of Behan's popularity is that he flouts convention with impunity and obvious glee. He takes a delight at cocking his nose at suburban respectability, at the smug reserve in which most of us wrap ourselves and at the stupidity of modern life which seems to reduce everyone to the same level of characterless nonentity.

*   *   *

Joan Littlewood found Brendan:

A fine scholar and a glorious clown . . . a man who took the world on a spree.

*   *   *

Flann O'Brien (Myles na gCopaleen) said after Brendan's death:

He was a delightful rowdy, a wit, a man of action in many dangerous undertakings where he thought his duty lay, a reckless drinker, a fearsome denouncer of humbug and pretence, and sole proprietor of the biggest heart that has beaten in Ireland over the past forty years.

*　　*　　*

Alan Brien in the Daily Telegraph:

He was a born soldier and exposed himself in many firing lines beyond the call of duty. To those of us who never took life neat, who watered our enthusiasms and diluted our passions to make them last longer, his great stomach for experience seemed sometimes foolhardy.

*　　*　　*

Frank O'Connor:

There glowed in Brendan the innocence of an accolyte.

*　　*　　*

René McColl in the Daily Express:

His is the story of F Scott-Fitzgerald all over again. The story of a brilliant man who simply can't keep off the bottle.

*　　*　　*

The Daily Mirror:

The boozy, roaring misfit, touched with genius; the charmer and the wit.

*   *   *

The Guardian:

Under the influence he could be as tiresome as the next man – but in his happier hours he was unaffected, generous, unfailingly entertaining and, whatever the faults of his plays, the themes reflected his essential humanity.

*   *   *

David Nathan of the Daily Herald *knew him as:*

The laughing story teller with the gap-toothed smile who was a far greater writer than he ever was a drinker. And a far greater man than either.

*   *   *

James Shannon, President of the Ancient Order of Hibernians in Chicago, said:

Too fast living, too hard living and a little out of the Irish concept of good moral living.

*   *   *

Sean O'Casey once was asked if he knew Brendan:

No, but I know all about him. I didn't know George Washington or Wolfe Tone but I knew all about them too.

*   *   *

Francis MacManus:

Where others preach and sermonise Behan jokes.

*   *   *

Brian Behan, Brendan's brother, wrote in his book With Chest Expanded:

I'm damn sure a world where the Brendans would rule would be a lot better than the stupid, crazy, chaotic one that we live in now. In the end there was nothing left for him to do but die, and everything else he did he carried it to excess.

*   *   *

Jimmy Breslin:

Behan is my set's idea of a real writer. For one thing, he drinks like a writer.

*   *   *

Harold Pinter met Brendan once:

He impressed me as a man with a blazing spirit. I thought he was a fine writer. He just didn't care a damn . . . that was his quality – and it was his wonderful sense of freedom that made us laugh.

*   *   *

W R Rodgers remembers a day Brendan arrived late for an appointment and when at last he burst in he was full of apologies and offering a story against himself as a reason for the delay:

I was rushing down Grafton Street when suddenly I knocked into a big woman in black from the country and I nearly drove her through Switzer's window. So I stopped and picked her up and dusted her down and I said to her: 'I'm sorry, ma'am, if I have inconvenienced you in any way and I hope no harm comes to you from this sad mis-adventure.' With that the big woman turns to the crowd gathered around us. 'There's still manners and courtesy left in the country,' she announced and then looked at me and added: 'Even from the lowest of the low.'

Drinking

The legend of Behan the drinker is almost as widely related as that of Behan the writer. He began to take 'a sup' early in life under the experienced eye of the Granny English and he graduated easily from the glass of cordial, given free to the children of the customers of Dublin's public houses, to the black, robust nourishment of Guinness. As a student drinker he made the acquaintance of almost every 'grocer's curate' – as Irish barmen were called – and in this way laid the foundations of the legends of a man who would drink, not just in pint glasses but in barrels, hogsheads, and swim in a sea of poteen and porter.

*   *   *

I never turned to drink, it seemed to turn to me. I don't ever remember not drinking.

*   *   *

I was practically born in the glass.

*   *   *

As a youngster I was a strict TT because I was a Stanley Woods fan and I thought it had something to do with the Isle of Man races.

*   *   *

Brendan recounted frequently the story of the first drop he ever tasted:

The older ladies believed in a sup of porter for children of pre-Confirmation age and used to say: 'Let them have a taste of it now and they'll never bother with it when they're grown up.' But, as it's proved, some theories have little or no scientific basis.

*   *   *

Another version of the same story:

I first learnt the use of whiskey at the age of six from my grandmother, who said: 'Give him the sup of it now, and he will never know the taste of it when he grows up,' which, I suppose, is the biggest understatement of all time; in my case anyway.

*   *   *

As regards the drink, I can only say that when I was growing up drunkenness was not regarded as a social disgrace. To get enough to eat was regarded as an achievement. To get drunk was a victory.

*   *   *

Drink is good enough any time of the day. I take it for breakfast, dinner and tea. No, that's a lie . . . I take a cuppa tea and a rasher sometimes but that's only to cod the wife.

*   *   *

Stout was the only drink he found good enough to follow the whiskey:

Whiskey is too good to be sullied with water.

*   *   *

Much the same theory he applied to soda-water:

A good drink invented in Dublin, but better with whiskey than straight.

*   *   *

Hangovers were few for Brendan. Life was almost a permanent drink. Asked by a radio interviewer how he could distinguish a hangover from the rest of his life, he said:

A hangover for me is when the brew of the night meets the dawn of the day.

* * *

Even the BBC wasn't immune to Behanism. Their switchboard was jammed with calls after Brendan appeared on Panorama. *Behan was surprised at the reaction:*

Yes, I had a few drinks. Everyone in Ireland knows that I take a drink and takes no notice. In Dublin the whole thing would have passed without comment.

* * *

Asked if he thought it was appropriate to appear drunk in front of BBC television cameras, he said:

I thought it perfectly natural. Yes, in my case, yes.

* * *

I only take a drink twice a day – when I'm thirsty and when I'm not.

* * *

In the matter of alcohol, principles are few.

* * *

A barman who worked in the 'Blue Lion' in Parnell Street remembers the time Brendan was told he owed ten shillings:

'For what?' he asked. 'You broke a glass the last time you were here,' we told him. 'God bless us,' he said, 'it must have been a very dear glass to cost ten shillings. Tell us, was it a Waterford glass or something?' He discovered quick enough that it wasn't a glass that you'd drink out of we meant – it was a pane of glass that he'd stuck somebody's head through!

*   *   *

Only the lower classes drink Scotch; it marks you off to go into a London pub and ask for Irish nowadays: when they've finished looking at you, they realise slowly that you've got a very eclectic palate.

*   *   *

I bought a decanter in the Daisy Market once – I'm very fond of decanters, I've a slight weakness for what goes into them.

*   *   *

I've always liked the story Brendan told about the two drunks that came out one evening to look for the grave of a friend of theirs.

They asked for Mulcahy of the Coombe and were told where he was buried. After traipsing about in the fog they found the grave, sure enough. One of the drunks spelt out the name: Terence Mulcahy. The other drunk was blinking up at a statue of Our Saviour the widow had got put up . . . and, after blinking up at the sacred figure, 'Not a bloody bit like himself,' says he, 'that's not Mulcahy, whoever done it.'

*   *   *

The one thing to the lasting credit of the British Navy is that it serves drink to its inmates and doesn't care about people being drunk.

*   *   *

Defending his return to drink after a spell 'on the wagon' Brendan said:

I'd be going against my doctor's orders if I drank milk, and I'd be going against my religion if I drank tea or coffee, and I'm just about to have something to eat and I need something to drink with my food.

*   *   *

Bars are usually the best places for a writer to go – most of them are full of poor people, hard-chaws, ex-convicts, chancers and tramps who'd lift the froth off your pint if you didn't keep your nose well in over the edge of the glass.

* * *

When pressed I will even drink with nobility.

* * *

I was drunk. I am usually half-shot and why not? I'm an enemy of the State – every damn State.

* * *

I was never able for American beer – me Granny made better.

* * *

Were you ever in McSorley's? The first McSorley wouldn't sell hard liquor and he wouldn't allow a woman in the place, and to this day, God love him, you will get a great pint of beer and an onion sandwich. But you get no malt or no mots.

* * *

In a New York night club Brendan was told a couple were dancing the Madison.

A bloody effective dance – I'd never seen it done before and after a jar or two I started doing the bloody thing meself.

* * *

There's a pub in Ringsend and it's all widows. Young widows, old widows, thin widows, fat widows, rich widows and poor widows. They sit there talking about their husbands all night, till nine o'clock, when they start crying over them. You might call the pub a boo-hoozer.

* * *

Once, in a Dublin public house, he was touched for a fiver by a gentleman with a nose for suckers. Behan turned him down curtly. 'I remember a time, Behan,' said the toucher, 'when you hadn't an effin' farthing to your name!'

That may be, but you don't remember it half as well as I do!

* * *

There's only one way to stop drinking – have your mouth full of the malt.

* * *

Outside Dublin's famous little Pike Theatre as the cast of The
Rose Tattoo *waited to be arrested for taking part in the play,
Brendan came on the scene. Immediately he sent up to Mooney's
pub for a crate of stout. Then as he distributed it among the
audience he said:*

Mind the bottles! They'll come in handy for ammunition.

*   *   *

Water's only any good for sailing ships on.

*   *   *

A methylated martyr, that's what I am.

*   *   *

*Brendan, at the height of his drunken notoriety, collapsed in a
diabetic coma in the streets of Dublin. Passers-by who thought he
was dead drunk deposited him in the nearest house, which happened to be the surgery of one of Dublin's most fashionable and
respected doctors. The doctor decided to take a cardiograph there
and then with Brendan lying on the couch. Somewhat nervous of
his patient, the doctor decided to humour him. He explained the
workings of the cardiograph needle as it registered the faint heart-
beats of the very sick and semi-conscious Brendan. 'That needle
there is writing down your pulses, Mr Behan, and I suppose in it's*

own way, it is probably the most important thing you have ever written!' To which Brendan replied:

Aye, and it's straight from me heart, too!

*   *   *

There he was, waiting for the barman to bring him a drink, and he with a face like a plateful of mortal sins.

*   *   *

I was up in the 'Blue Lion' the other morning and there was this oul' one sitting opposite me, looking at me like a sow looking into a swill barrel.

*   *   *

When I was starting to drink a pint cost seven pence – and, be Jasus, it was different to the stuff that costs four times as much today. It would stick to the counter if you left it there for sixty seconds.

*   *   *

You'll never find high-up civil servants drinking under their own names.

*   *   *

If you ever go across the bogs to Galway don't let anyone talk you into drinking the poteen. A torchlight procession would be easier to swallow.

*   *   *

Mr C A Joyce, his former Borstal governor, got constant calls from Brendan through the years . . . and at the most unearthly hours. One night Mrs Joyce answered a past-midnight call. 'Brendan dear,' she said, 'will you go back to bed and phone about ten in the morning.' To which Brendan replied:

I can't, sure that's drinking time in Ireland.

*   *   *

It takes a lot of talk to fill a pint.

*   *   *

John B Keane, playwright and publican, relates the story of his young son, Billy, who was sitting on Brendan's knee. Already Brendan had had plenty to drink. 'Don't drink any more,' advised little Billy.

Whatever you say, Bill, whatever you say, but I'll just have to have one more to wash down the last one.

*   *   *

The only good turn drink ever did for Brendan Francis Behan was the popularisation of the said Brendan Francis Behan.

*　　*　　*

I drink like a fish – the only difference is that we drink different stuff.

*　　*　　*

Once asked on a Radio Eireann interview how he was going to spend New Year's Eve he replied:

Like any other day – ebbing and flowing. Ebbing in the morning and flowing in the evening.

*　　*　　*

Talking in a New York bar:

A club in Canada has offered me a thousand dollars to go up there and sing – for doing the same in Dublin I get thrown out of pubs.

*　　*　　*

Writing in The People *from a hospital bed after one of his earlier drinking bouts:*

The nurse has warned me that if I let this typewriter fall and frighten the patient beside me she'll break the water jug on my head. God forgive her! I have a baby bottle of whiskey hidden in it.

*   *   *

I drink beer because a pint of orange juice is twice the price of a pint of stout.

An Amiable Person

Brendan would never agree that he was a fighting man . . . yet this is just as much part of the image of Behan as the writing and the drinking. He was raised at a time and in a part of Dublin where 'only a fool was too proud to fight and only a bloody fool would pretend he was afraid'. The accumulation of court appearances were mostly for drunkenness but sometimes they were accompanied by an assault charge. The headlines tell the story to the world: 'Behan fined in Toronto'; 'Behan banned in New York'; 'London spree cost Behan £150'. There were other ones too that told of the term he spent in Borstal and prison on charges of being a member of the IRA. He summed them all up in a few well-chosen words . . . 'It's better to be fighting than to be lonely.' But at the same time he knew well his own potential.

*   *   *

I'm a gentle and amiable person.

*   *   *

I'm the most captured soldier in Irish history.

*   *   *

I'm not a warlike man – as a matter of fact a highly ineffectual one. The IRA had sufficient good military sense never to make me more than a messenger boy.

*   *   *

The famed British reserve is as much a myth as the idea of the broth-of-a-boy Irishman, the fella of the ready wit and the warm heart and the great love for a fight.

*   *   *

I hate policemen – whether they are Irish, British or Russian.

*   *   *

On the big island of Aran I was in company with two fishermen, and one night we imprisoned the island's police force, which consisted of two guards, in their own cells and threw the keys down the cliffs. We didn't do this without some provocation, because they had come in to arrest us for singing a song in the village street.

*   *   *

I don't respect the law – it doesn't seem to have much respect for me.

*   *   *

The cops, the guards, the gendarmes – call them what you like – I have a different collective name for them. They are mostly culchies, a word most people would recognise better as peasants. They are delighted to be let loose on towns in uniforms and with guns, through whose streets they crawled in dumb wondering fear when first they left the bogs.

*   *   *

Only a lunatic boasts of taking human life.

*   *   *

'*We were in the same brigade in the IRA,*' *a young man shouted to all and sundry. Behan suddenly sobered and took a long, hard look at the newcomer.*

Go 'long, you bowsie! The only brigade you ever saw was the Fire Brigade.

*   *   *

Ireland – and especially Phoenix Park – is full of statues,

mainly of British generals. The IRA spent a good deal of their time trying to blow them up – a harmless enough occupation, in fact a bit like their sentencing me to death once in my absence: I sent them back a polite note saying that they could shoot me in my absence also.

*   *   *

It's better to be defiant – in a quiet sort of way.

*   *   *

'*We were listening to an elderly character boasting about his part in the 1916 Rebellion and making exaggerated claims,*' remembers *Iohn Murdoch.*

Voice Number One, gruffly: Where were you in 1916?
Voice Number Two, softly: I wasn't anywhere in 1916; I wasn't born until 1920.
Voice Number One, with contemptuous sarcasm: Oh excuses! Always excuses!

*   *   *

There was a similar situation in McDaids of Harry Street, where a loud-mouthed individual was addressing imbibers on his achievements as a freedom fighter. Exasperated, Brendan got up from his seat, walked over to the individual at the counter and roared at him:

You are far too young to have died for Ireland!

*   *   *

Did you see in the paper that fourteen thousand ex-IRA men walked through Chicago wearing IRA sashes? As an ex-member of the IRA I have to tell you that I've never seen an IRA sash, but if there had been that number of men in the IRA we'd have taken back the Isle of Man, not to mention the Six Counties.

*   *   *

On one occasion an IRA man was to be 'rescued' from Leyhill prison in Surrey and it was Brendan's job after the rescue to guard a Park Ranger in the vicinity of the prison.

A decent man. A quiet respectable Irishman who, even though he was employed by the British Imperial Majesty, never spoke a word against us or his parent country. Helpful, not a bit of trouble. And the only effin' thing I did to convince him of our good intentions was to hold a .45 revolver at his head all the time. Cocked.

*   *   *

Brendan often said that he was not proud of his early life.

I don't like violence, but I was a soldier. If you'd seen as much as I did you'd agree with Shaw, who said when he was asked what he felt about the Republican Army's method of fighting the British Army: 'A perambulator hasn't much choice of tactics against a furniture van.'

*　　　*　　　*

He was an expert with explosives and had a few words to say about bombs.

Why are the Irish or even a section of the Irish the only ones not permitted to use bombs? Is it because we only use little ones and the others use big ones?

*　　　*　　　*

I always carried gelignite; dynamite isn't safe.

*　　　*　　　*

The only man I ever heard admit he'd been in the Black and Tans was a Liverpool fella who explained that he joined because he hadn't the fare for the Foreign Legion.

*　　　*　　　*

The Irish who fought for Franco had the remarkable military feat of coming home with more men than they went out with.

*　　　*　　　*

One of Brendan's favourite stories, remembers Michael O'Connell, was about the woman who boasted that her husband was a 'ral' in the British forces. When eventually someone asked her what a 'ral' was she said:

It's either an admiral, a general or a corporal. Sure, even the poor devil himself isn't sure.

Court and Prison

Over six years of Brendan's short life were spent in prison. Being gregarious he found it very hard. In Borstal Boy *he records how he hoped the warders would come and open his door even if it was to do nothing better than to give him a few knocks and thumps. Even the rough company of the prison was better than solitude. All his best writing came like a roar of laughter from the cells of Strangeways in Manchester, Mountjoy in Dublin and the Glasshouse in the Curragh.*

Being the man he was he even had the governors of the prisons awaiting his arrival with interest. But as Sean Kavanagh, one-time governor of Mountjoy, wrote in The World of Brendan Behan: *'But meeting this mild-mannered boy gave one a feeling of anti-climax; surely this was no desperado, no trigger-happy gunman.' Later Mr Kavanagh classified Brendan as 'the second untidiest prisoner he ever knew'. But if prison governors found him mild Brendan didn't feel the same about prison.*

* * *

Mountjoy, Regina Coeli, Sing Sing are very good names

for prisons, but there are few places named more appropri-
ately than Strangeways.

* * *

I was in the Joy myself often enough to be President of
Ireland three times over.

* * *

*'Which prison do you prefer – English or Irish?' asked an
interviewer.*

English jails when you're young and Irish jails when you
are older.

* * *

'He came to me,' relates Borstal governor, Mr C A Joyce,
'one day and said: "You must understand, sir, that the freedom of Ireland is to me a second religion." '

* * *

The famous police-shooting incident occurred on Easter
Sunday, 5th April 1942, and on the 24th of that month
Brendan appeared before a military court and was sentenced
quickly to fourteen years on one charge and three months
on another. With characteristic good humour he asked the

presiding officer if he could take his pick as he preferred the three months' sentence.

*   *   *

I was serving a sentence during the war in Ireland for attempting to murder two policemen – but, by Jasus, they weren't charged with a prior attempt to murder me.

*   *   *

There was a fellow in prison whose lawyer was known to boast that he got him a suspended sentence. They hanged him.

*   *   *

Brendan was being defended on a charge of entering England illegally. His solicitor apologised for his behaviour and put it down to him being a 'love child of the Irish revolution'. Grinning a toothless grin at the memory he would relate:

The mother was scandalised, never mind slandered.

*   *   *

Although you mightn't agree with me, in Ireland there is such a thing as an honourable murder charge.

*   *   *

Whenever the English put me in prison I knew exactly what to do. Talk well to the ones that mattered and have an answer ready for the screws I didn't like – this answer was always historically informed and obscene.

*   *   *

It wasn't always quiet in the cells – some fellas made so much noise that you'd think they were getting birdseed with their bread and water.

*   *   *

Nowadays you'd almost be needing to go to jail before you'd be accepted as a bloody writer.

*   *   *

Benedict Kiely once remarked to Brendan that if the cost of living got any higher in Dublin he himself would land up in prison for debt. With affected horror Brendan spluttered:

Don't take away from me the one advantage I have in this hard-backed business.

*   *   *

He told a court:

My.whole system is upset by the sight of a police uniform.

*　　　*　　　*

Once he offered to go bail for £250 in a Dublin court. Asked by the judge if this was all right – after all it was a large sum of money – Brendan replied:

I've been speaking to the prisoner and impressed on him that while I am not a notorious upholder of the law I am a notorious upholder of my £250.

*　　　*　　　*

Offering bail for another friend in 1961 Brendan apologised to the court:

For the fact that I have not shaved and that I have not got a tie on. It is not out of disrespect for you but I was engaged this morning dictating a new play in Irish, *La Breagh San Roilig* ('A fine day in the graveyard'), and I did not expect to spend '*La breagh sa Chuirt*' ('A fine day in the Court').

*　　　*　　　*

A man due to be hanged asked Brendan if hanging hurt. Brendan assured him with his own special brand of kindness that he didn't think so but he couldn't guarantee:

I've never been through it myself nor have I spoken to anyone who has.

*   *   *

'Brendan, like Lord Byron,' says Benedict Kiely, 'woke up one morning and found himself famous. He had written *The Quare Fellow* and it came up right in the middle of the English debate on capital punishment. "And that," said Brendan, "was the only good turn hanging ever did to me or anyone else." '

*   *   *

Paying a fine for a friend in a Dublin court:

I regard this as an investment in humanity.

A Daylight Atheist

Many of the phrases in Brendan's vocabulary were prefaced by 'bejaysus', which many considered was taking the Lord's name in vain. I once asked Liam Dwyer, who Brendan called 'the other half of me', about this: 'A priest once asked me the same question,' he said, 'and I told him that it's His friends who know him by His first name.' No doubt the Behan reply would have been much the same. His own famous reply about his religious views was that he wasn't a daylight Catholic but when it got dark he was liable to change his mind.

*   *   *

The teacher often said she was never sure what religion I was, although all belonging to me were Catholics since AD 432.

*   *   *

I'm a bad Catholic, it's the religion of great artists.

*   *   *

I'm a bad Catholic, like many another great artist, like Rabelais and Michelangelo.

* * *

If people want me to behave like Cardinal Spellman or Billy Graham, why don't they pay me the salary those fellows are getting?

* * *

'What's the Ascendancy?' someone once asked him, and Brendan replied:

A Protestant on a horse.

* * *

When I'm in health I'm not at all religious. But when I'm sick I'm very religious.

* * *

The Catholic background came in defence of the Old Faith when Brendan told Hannen Swaffer, the columnist, who had just announced that he was a spiritualist:

Catholicism keeps a better type of ghost.

* * *

Pound notes are the best religion in the world.

*   *   *

After a friend of his died he said:

The nuns will be comforted to know he'd no mortal sin on his soul; none at least to keep him longer than a few short years of harmonious torture in Purgatory.

*   *   *

Did you ever hear the story of Daddy Crowe, who went to visit the Pope. He didn't kiss the Pope's ring – he took him by the hand, shook it heartily and said: 'Jasus, Holy Father, there's not a man in Limerick that wouldn't go to hell for you.'

*   *   *

'What's your business, matey?' he asked of the Bishop of Knaresborough. 'Not so profitable as yours, I'm afraid,' came the answer.

And Brendan, never slow to give credit, always laughed when he told how he acknowledged the Bishop's wit with a hearty handshake that caused the older man to wince.

*   *   *

New York has a church to cater for everybody, just as it has a night club to cater for everybody.

* * *

Once describing a frightening experience Brendan said:

Not all the sins of my past life passed in front of me, but as many as could get room in the queue. Not since I slept in a barn next to a horse that mended his own shoes in the small hours of the morning, was I so frightened.

* * *

Mr Ernest Blythe, former managing director of the Abbey Theatre, remembers the time Brendan went around saying that the well-known poet, Paddy Kavanagh, was so pro-British that he was going around saying that Edward VII was a Catholic!

* * *

There was a theologian who saw hell as an empty place but unfortunately for all our peace of minds that was in 1740 – things may well have changed since.

* * *

In religion my family has always been Catholic – and anti-clerical. I don't know of one priest in any generation of the family and I don't know of one member of it who has died without a priest. *Deo Gratias.*

Politics

Very early in life Brendan was whipped into the passionate tide of freedom which, for so many at the time, meant the IRA. It can be said that this form of activity was more militant than political, but it certainly left a mark on the growing boy who once said that the IRA had 'the good sense never to make me more than a messenger boy'. But a plant never changes from a shamrock to a rose and all through his life Brendan stuck to his early beliefs. He had little time for Irish politics or politicians although some of the leading figures in government often spoke in his favour.

*   *   *

Behan was in New York shortly after Mr F H Boland had been elected President of the UN General Assembly. Mr Boland was going in to see the first performance of Behan's The Hostage *when he met Brendan in the foyer. Their conversation went this way:*

Mr Behan: I opened a show tonight.
Mr Boland: I also opened a show tonight.

Mr Behan: How did your show go?
Mr Boland: Quite well. How did yours go?
Mr Behan: I'll ring you tomorrow morning and tell you.

*   *   *

I'm not a politician. I've only got one face.

*   *   *

Brendan once said that a woman he knew well had two sons:

One of them is a politician, the other is an honest individual.

*   *   *

If anybody over the age of twenty-five gets a heart attack over politics they deserve to have one.

*   *   *

Everybody in Ireland is against partition, it has me in the same camp as the Prime Minister – and I don't want to be in the same camp as the Taoiseach any more than he wants to be in the same camp as meself.

*   *   *

I think I'm as well behaved as most politicians, owners of television networks, newspaper proprietors. I'm not dead and I don't belong to posterity yet. How's my health? If I felt any better I couldn't stand it.

*　　*　　*

Some people boast they've friends on both sides of politics. I'm proud to have enemies on both sides.

*　　*　　*

To a well-known journalist Brendan once said:

Well, I know you've got very good clothes and obviously you didn't come by them honestly, but on the other hand I know you aren't a politician, because you look too bloody honest.

*　　*　　*

When somebody asked him on a television show what he thought of the Irish politically in America, he said:

It depends on whether you mean the late Senator McCarthy or Mrs Elizabeth Gurley Flynn.

*　　*　　*

The man was sweeping the street outside the Irish Press *office and he asked Brendan who was going to win an election. His reply:*

Whoever gets in, you'll still be sweeping the street.

*　　*　　*

In the 1959 election Brendan wanted to work for Dr Noel Browne – but the politician's supporters were worried at the possible outcome of Brendan's 'support'. But he soon stopped the worries:

I'll tell you what I'll do – I'll canvas for the other fella . . . that'll be enough to win the election for Browne.

*　　*　　*

A New York judge banned him from the St Patrick's Day parade in 1961 and described him as a disorderly person. But Brendan wasn't worried:

The judge is in a tough position . . . but then it's a bit of publicity for him. It's election year for judges.

*　　*　　*

J P Murray, the humorist, remembers that shortly after returning from America Brendan told him of the minor role he played in the Kennedy Presidential Election Campaign. With a party of electioneers he went canvassing for votes in a small American town:

To his amazement he met a group of about twenty old ladies who spoke fluent Gaelic. They had emigrated to the States years ago but had managed to preserve their native language. They were devout Catholic ladies but were Nixon supporters! (From here on Brendan told me the story in Gaelic.) They were voting for Nixon, they said, because, although he was not a Roman Catholic like themselves and Kennedy, he looked a very decent man. And was also handsome. It would be useless to talk political policies to such dear dedicated old ladies, but Brendan hit them where it hurt most, and in their own native language he asked them: 'Did ye not hear what Nixon said about our Holy Father the Pope?' The old ladies were deeply shocked and concerned. 'Tell us, Brendan, son, what did that blackguard Nixon say about poor Pope John?' And luckily, before Brendan had time to reply, the campaign truck drove off and left them wondering. And that, said Brendan to me, was a sure twenty votes, for Kennedy!

*　　*　　*

An air hostess called to the passengers as the plane came in to land. 'We are coming into Dublin,' she said, 'please tighten your belts.' From the back came the voice of Brendan:

Let's leave politics outa this.

*　　*　　*

Describing a woman who had been defeated in an election:

She was so disappointed that she looked like a woman who looked under her bed hoping to find a man there but only found a collar stud.

*　　*　　*

The days of levelling the up hills of Ireland to leave the down hills the way they are went out with John Bull.

*　　*　　*

Wrote Brendan in the Irish Press:

I remember the puckered grin of the tough old republican from West Clare who was asked whether his fight for Ireland had benefited him personally. 'I got,' he said, 'forty acres of this country. Forty acres when the tide is out.'

Ireland and the Irish

If there was one thing that Brendan could be contradictory about it was his own country and his own countrymen. There was many a time when he wished: 'I could let the Isle of the Blest see only the heels of me trotters' and many another time when he went the width and breadth of Ireland singing the glories of the land with all his bawdy gusto. Some of this love and disillusionment seeped into Brendan Behan's Island *and into the collected* Irish Press *columns* Hold your Hour and Have Another. *Typical of his love of the land was his comment that in Ireland 'every hour of Irish sunshine is like the Lord polishing up his own decanter'. On a fine day he would say: 'It's the sort of day you'd know that Christ died for you.' Then in a typical twist he would remind you: 'A bloody good job I was born in rainy Ireland and not in the South of France or California where I'd have been so bloody grateful and holy for the sunshine that Saint Paul would only have been trotting after me.'*

*   *   *

This country is a combination of chemical elements called Ireland.

*   *   *

Someone said to Brendan: 'Do you know you could do a lot for this country and you could do a lot with this country.' To which he replied:

Well, you could blow it up.

Then after a brief pause:

You can take that remark more as the humour of the moment than my permanent attitude.

*　　　*　　　*

Sure God help the Irish, if it was raining soup, we'd be out with forks.

*　　　*　　　*

In a moment of despair in New York he told an interviewer:

I regard Ireland in the same way as Sean O'Casey. It's a great country to get a letter from.

*　　　*　　　*

Courageous the man who attacked or even innocently said a wrong word about Ireland in Brendan's presence. Once hearing someone comment on 'Eire' he jumped up and attacked:

My country's Ireland. It's an impertinence to call it Eire. If you are referring to Germany, you wouldn't say that you made a trip to Deutschland or that you drank Deutsch wine.

*　　*　　*

I have never ridiculed my Faith, but as regards my Fatherland the first duty of a writer is to let his Fatherland down, otherwise he is no writer. In the name of Jesus, how the hell can a writer attack anyone else's Fatherland if he doesn't attack his own?

*　　*　　*

Ireland has been cursed with gentlemen farmers – they're men who raise nothing except their hats . . . and only do that to Protestant clergymen.

*　　*　　*

There's some Irish would eat cooked Kenyan if they thought 'the quality' in England were doing the same.

*　　*　　*

'Ireland is civilisation,' said Brendan on a New York radio show. 'What reasons do you give for this?' asked the interviewer. 'A pop singer can make a fortune there and a poet can starve.'

*　　*　　*

If there were only three Irishmen left in the world you'd find two of them in a corner talking about the other. We're a backbiting race.

*   *   *

My own people – the Irish – won't accept me, but they'll take my bloody money.

*   *   *

Every nationality has persecuted somebody at some time or another. Even we should remember that when Saint Patrick came over to Ireland he was brought as a slave by and for the Irish.

*   *   *

I've plenty of respect for my fellow Irish. They're my raw material. I write about them. I immortalise them.

*   *   *

The Irish that I know are the Irish I like, the ordinary ones, taxi-drivers, house-painters, bookies' runners. . . . I don't say honest workers – some of them are extremely dishonest workers – but they're the people I care about. And in any country they don't buy books very much and they don't live by books or by literature, except newspapers with the

Brendan the mimic, giving his unique impression of an old
woman from the 'back end of Galway'.

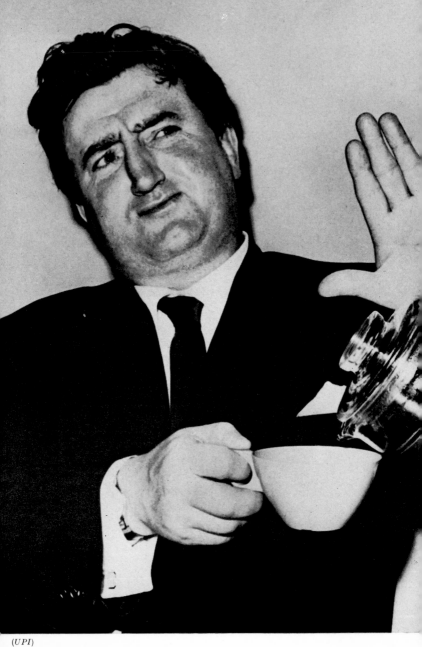

No black coffee! This was Los Angeles in 1961 – seven days
after Brendan's conviction for being drunk and disorderly.

racing results. The theatre-going people, what passes for society, I don't like and they don't like me.

*   *   *

It's the working class that binds me to Ireland; they're the only real people here. The middle classes put years on me.

*   *   *

Brendan's gregarious nature showed itself time after time. Talking about his home town he said:

In Dublin you have conviviality, but no friendship. And Dublin will give you loneliness too – but no solitude.

*   *   *

Louis Armstrong said when I asked him what he thought of Dublin: 'What's Dublin?' he said. 'Can you play it?'

*   *   *

The Dubliner is the victim of his own prejudices.

*   *   *

When he couldn't afford a taxi Brendan had to depend on Dublin's buses:

The only times I ever knew the buses of Dublin to go fast is when I'm running to get on one.

*   *   *

The Guinness family have always been very good to the people of Dublin but as one fella said: 'The people of Dublin are very kind to the Guinnesses.'

*   *   *

Quoting a famous Dublin toilet-wall message was one of Brendan's favourite pastimes:

You pull the chain and, in a jiffey, your shit is floating down the Liffey.

Then he often added:

Somebody once said that Joyce made the Liffey the Ganges of the literary world, but sometimes the smell of the Ganges of the literary world is not all that literary.

*   *   *

Kilbarrack, over by Howth, my father always maintained, was the healthiest graveyard in the country, with the sea air.

*   *   *

Anglo-Irishmen only work at riding horses, drinking whiskey and reading double-meaning books in Irish at Trinity College – No I'm telling you a lie, there's no such thing as an Anglo-Irishman as Shaw pointed out – except as a class distinction.

*   *   *

Since I was a child I've had a pathological horror of country people.

*   *   *

Cork is a delightful land of pig meat and porter.

*   *   *

Limerick girls are very careful about keeping their legs shut, if not their mouths.

*   *   *

The great thing I have discovered about Orangemen is that they have feelings.

*   *   *

In the Boyne Tavern in the Shankill Road, the Protestant part of Belfast, they called on Brendan for a song and, as he retold the story:

As cute as a Christian, what do you think I sang? 'Put More Turf on the Fire, Mary Anne.' Discretion was the better part of valour. Though the company were decent Protestant workers, you never know what half-fool is lying in the background waiting to make a name for himself by crowning the stranger with a porter bottle – you get them everywhere.

*   *   *

In the North of Ireland I'm sometimes regarded as a crypto-Sinn Feiner and in the South it is the official party line that I'm an atheist.

*   *   *

Sitting in a bus going near Belfast a passenger told Brendan that they were between Purdysburn Mental Hospital and the Government buildings at Stormont.

From which I construed we were passing between misery and madness.

*   *   *

The Irish are a very popular race – with themselves.

America and the Americans

Everyone needs a second land – Brendan found his on the other side of the Atlantic duck-pond. Nowhere else, not even France, was as attractive to him as the United States. He loved New York next to Dublin, the times he took himself there he was at his best – and his worst. From the Chelsea Hotel right through the bars to the theatres and courtrooms – they all saw Brendan. And now and again Brendan saw them for all they were.

*   *   *

In a letter to the New Yorker *he made a list of the things he most wanted to do:*

I would like to see the Rockefeller paintings by Diego Rivera. I would also like to meet in New York the Rockefeller who said that he would like to see me in Ireland. I would like to see and pay my respect to Big Daddy Burl Ives, Lee Tracy, Studs Lonigan, Billy Graham, Tom Lehrer, the Empire State Building, the St Patrick's Day parade on Fifth Avenue, Costello's saloon on Third Avenue, Robert

Frost, Marilyn Monroe, back and front, the most unforget-table character you know, the Mafia, the Mizrachi, the Daughters of the American Revolution, the Ivy League, Niagara Falls, Nick the Greek, the Governor's pitch in Albany, William Faulkner, the Yankee Stadium, a love nest, a hot-dog stand, a jam session, the Golden Gloves, and the candidates for the presidential election.

*   *   *

If I had the chance of sweeping the streets of Broadway or being Lord Mayor of Shrewsbury, I think I would sweep the streets of Broadway. It would be more fun.

*   *   *

The public transport in New York is so bad that Dublin's green double-decker buses would be a sensation on Fifth Avenue.

*   *   *

Vassar College is my Tir na n-Og (my land of eternal youth).

*   *   *

New York's taxi-drivers try to live up to the reputation that all taxi-drivers have, of being wits. As I am in the wit business myself, I object to competition, even from taxi-drivers.

*　　*　　*

New York is easily recognisable as the greatest city in the world: look at it any way and every way – back, belly and sides.

London is a wide flat pie of redbrick suburbs with the West End stuck in the middle like a currant. New York is a huge rich raisin and is the biggest city I can imagine.

*　　*　　*

If I were skint, I would sooner be skint on the Bowery than in Westchester County. It is more civilised and the conversation is better, but I would prefer the Algonquin or the Hotel Chelsea to either place.

*　　*　　*

I met a lot of nice people in Hollywood. The only trouble was keeping tabs on who was married to who. When a girl marries there she throws the bridegroom away before she throws the bouquet.

And later:

It's the land of permanent waves and impermanent wives.

*　　*　　*

To go to California and not see Hollywood is like going to Ireland and not seeing the Lakes of Killarney.

*　　*　　*

California is the place to live. New York is the greatest city in the world, but six months a year in California is just what I want.

*　　*　　*

Do you know how the Americans spell money? R-o-c-k-e-f-e-l-l-e-r.

*　　*　　*

The art of conversation has been murdered by lunatics, mostly from the United States.

*　　*　　*

Only Americans think America is important; no one else does.

*　　*　　*

If you're honest you go to America to earn a fortune; if you're a criminal you have to go farther – to Australia.

*　　*　　*

The only sort of man that most American women want to marry is the fella with a will of his own – made out in her favour.

*   *   *

New York is a very great city. It has its faults but anyone who dislikes it just does not like the human race. And Broadway is the big apple. There's no place like it – I did not tell the Americans that in case it would make them conceited. They're conceited enough already.

*   *   *

New York is hell . . . but I like it so much I must be a devil myself.

*   *   *

An extraordinary thing usually happens to me in the United States on St Patrick's Day. In Boston I got a police escort and the officer said to me: 'I suppose you get an escort in your own country, too.' I said, 'I must. I'm usually handcuffed there.'

*   *   *

In America the Paddys become Richards in three generations.

*   *   *

America worries too much about its colour problem – there's no such thing. The only really white man I've ever seen was a dead one.

* * *

New York:

I think the housing for the working classes here is lousy. Dublin city puts you to shame. The buses are small and filthy in comparison to our buses, and the subway is a death-trap. The newspapers, too, are effin' awful.

* * *

When it was suggested that Americans were broadminded because they put on a show of paintings by Picasso, 'a Communist', Brendan replied:

It does nothing of the sort. It only shows that you aren't able to do the bloody paintings as well as Picasso!

* * *

There are two things on which the Americans and the Russians might well join forces – first, to make people know as much at eighteen as they do at thirty-eight; and, second, to make people as attractive-looking at thirty-eight or forty-eight as they were at eighteen.

* * *

Greenwich Village is the only genuine Latin Quarter left in either Western Europe or any place else that I know. It is reputedly full of involved sex, and, of course, there is vice there.

There is vice in London and there is vice in Paris, and in Reykjavik and in East Jesus, Kansas. You can get vice anywhere, but the only exciting thing I found in the Village was when some fellow offered me a smoke of marijuana.

*   *   *

After a successful trip to New York:

I feel like a lonely flea that just found a dog.

England and the English

'*If it's worth visiting I've visited it,*' *said Brendan once when someone was talking about the beauties of England. Asked where he'd been he replied:* '*I know a few places very well – Holyhead, London, Liverpool, Harrogate and Strangeways.*' *He recounted once in his* Irish Press *column how he was asked what he thought of England.* '*I did not like, for politeness sake, to give a straight answer.*' *Politeness wasn't always his strong point and his feelings for England were mainly historic . . . certainly they were always said with feeling – as any of the staff at Dun Laoghaire, the North Wall or Dublin Airport will tell you.*

*   *   *

The English always have their wars in someone else's country.

*   *   *

The English are like the Germans, their first cousins, a

very innocent race of people. Gentle when they're taken away from their guns, their Queen, their kings.

*   *   *

Queen Victoria practically owned respectability.

*   *   *

My racial prejudices are nil – well, practically – because when I read about the Famine or the Easter Week Rising I get a bit bitter against England and the English.

*   *   *

Queen Victoria did one good deed during the Irish famine – she gave five pounds to the Relief Fund. But so as not to cause jealousy she gave five pounds on the same day to Battersea Dogs' Home.

*   *   *

Most people look upon the English as being a very sober race, but I know a lot of them who, I would say, have a stiff upper lip mostly because they are 'stiff' twenty-four hours a day.

*   *   *

I prefer to live in Ireland, but I've a great admiration for the British people. No one else could have used Churchill so well during the war and then thrown him out at the right time afterwards.

*   *   *

After The Hostage *had been chosen by the French director of the International Theatre Festival to represent Great Britain, Brendan said:*

Those limey suckers can't resist a spot of culture, first they put me in jail and then they make me famous. They take the bombs as well as the plays from out of me pocket!

*   *   *

The English are suckers. They give me nearly all my drinking money.

*   *   *

There's more difference between a Liverpudlian and a Cockney than there is between a Belfast man and a Dublin man. On the strength of these differences, there's more justification for partitioning England than there is for partitioning Ireland.

*   *   *

The English, God help them, expect every language to be like their own.

*　　　*　　　*

The varieties of English spoken in Liverpool, Harrogate or Somerset are outlandish enough for anyone's lifetime.

*　　　*　　　*

He was always glad and grateful that London gave him his first and best welcome as a playwright and that once when on the way through England from Ireland to France he was arrested under a deportation order the British authorities deported him not back to Ireland but onwards to France, paying his fare:

A humorous and decent people.

*　　　*　　　*

The English are even more subtle liars than we are.

*　　　*　　　*

The person on the bench, the magistrate, was, they told me, a gentle English Tory, which to me is like talking about a tame duck, dry water or a poor publican. She had a face like Harris Tweed.

*　　　*　　　*

Unless you are a policeman, a criminal or a prostitute, you have no business in Piccadilly after midnight.

*   *   *

England is full of discomforts, bad liquor, public houses without lavatories or telephones, and it's full of Irish, Welsh and Scots bogmen and English village idiots.

*   *   *

In his Irish Press *column:*

I am writing this in Bayswater, which is quite a pleasant mid-Victorian suburb, one of the residential areas of the great manufacturing bourgeoisie and now famous for its murders.

*   *   *

England is a very good place if you're sick, if you're old, or if you're rearing children, because the Health Act is a great thing. But the shutting of the pubs, for instance, every five minutes, I find somewhat disconcerting.

*   *   *

For all they looted and robbed, the English made considerably less use of the swag than smaller imperialisms.

*   *   *

Brendan sleeps while some of his relatives watch a rehearsal
of his brother Dominic's play *Posterity Be Damned* –
London, 1960.

Brendan Behan – 1923–1964.

London's such a dismal place that seeing my play there can't make it any more dismal.

* * *

The West End was made for me, not me for the West End.

Canada and the Canadians

One country that incensed Brendan more than any other – even England – was Canada. He couldn't, he said, find adjectives strong enough to describe it – and then went ahead in his own roaring way to vent his feelings on a land that wasn't absolutely Behan-crazy. Lectures and personal appearances were cancelled by various Canadian bodies when Brendan went on one of his skites. Soon he was in hospital. From Toronto to Ireland came the wired story 'Behan died today in hospital'. He refuted the story himself, sitting up in a hospital bed, praying hands holding a cigar and shouting: 'I'm not dead – only drunk.' But it didn't stop him adding his own candid comments about a short chapter of a short life.

*　　　*　　　*

On arrival at Cork after his fairly disastrous tour of Canada:

I felt so strongly about those bloody Canadians that when they took me into a Toronto hospital I had to think twice before I let them give me a local anaesthetic.

*　　　*　　　*

After his illness in Toronto he left the hospital and told the nurses he wanted to get out of this little country:

I have no desire to bolster the sagging cultural economy of this country.

* * *

Saying he banned all his plays being produced on Canadian television he said:

You can't have it both ways . . . you can't treat me the way you did and use my works too. It's a case of 'love me, love my dog'.

* * *

Taverns in Canada:

They were the places I really liked – but they wouldn't let my wife in.

* * *

Anyone who comes to Canada should bring his own home with him.

* * *

Ireland will put a shillelagh into orbit, Israel will put a matzo ball into orbit, and Liechtenstein will put a postage stamp into orbit before the Canadians put up a mouse.

*   *   *

Canada:

A lot of people say I hate Canada. I don't hate any place . . . well, I make certain exceptions. Canada's the only place where I've been accused of being a Dogan. That's an Irish Catholic. I asked them for it in writing so I could show it at home.

*   *   *

Toronto:

I got a lot of dough there. It'll be a marvellous city . . . it's only because I've a show there I'm saying that.

*   *   *

Montreal:

The only place where a good French accent isn't a social asset.

*   *   *

Vancouver:

A terrible hole.

* * *

Hamilton:

I can't be blasphemous enough about it.

Continong – and Continontals

'Like many another,' said Brendan, 'I'm just back from the Continong.' The only difference when Brendan said it was he generally meant France, although he also regarded Sweden as an outer suburb of Dublin. France though was where it all began. It was here 'I rounded off my missed education' in the 1940s; it was here he acquired considerable fluency in French and began writing ('mostly dirty stories or, if you like, little bits of pornography'), mainly for Points and Merlin, two Left Bank reviews. Lyons, Paris, Cannes all attracted him – and especially the Mediterranean, where you could get iced beer for one and ninepence and the whole shimmering sea all the way to Africa for nothing. His best writing of some of these visits appeared in the Irish Press and one told of his visit with Beatrice, his wife, to Amiens. 'Amm-ee-ah, what's that?' Beatrice is supposed to have said.

'Amm-ee-ah. The place between here and Paris.'
'It's Ameyens. A-m-i-e-n-s.'
'Yes, but it is pronounced "Amm-ee-ah".'
'Listen, if we ever get home and thaw ourselves out in the Gulf Stream well enough to walk, just try walking up to a

Guard in Talbot Street and ask him to direct you to Amm-ee-ah Street Station!'

However, in the heels of the hunt we got to the railway station of Saint Lazare.

In the course of the next few days I showed my wife the Opera and the Louvre. She said, when I said, 'See that, that's the Eiffel Tower', that her sight, thanks be to God, was not so bad that she would be likely to miss the tallest object in Europe at a distance of ten yards.

In return, when we did get home and tottered off the B and I and got three-quarters way up the North Wall, she brought me round the corner of Store Street and pointed. 'See that?' she asked.

I said I did.

'Well,' said she, 'that's Amm-ee-ah Street Station.'

*   *   *

I like France. They entertained me last year. France is led by madmen, gangsters and collaborators.

*   *   *

France disgraced herself in Algeria. The *colon* is a class of simple-minded Orangemen not particularly vicious in himself, but supported by the French right wing.

*   *   *

Saint Germain-des-Prés has replaced Montmartre as a refuge of sinners and intellectuals, genius and phoney.

*   *   *

The talk about local politicians and other notabilities in a Paris bistro is like a breath of home to the Dubliner, far from the scurrilities of pub conversation on his own native heath, and just as intimately savage.

*   *   *

The greatest possession an Irishman can have in Paris – besides his Irish passport – is a hard neck.

*   *   *

Brendan liked to repeat a story that he credited to Desmond Francis Ryan, about Marshal MacMahon, who was being interviewed shortly after being installed as President of the Third Republic. The question of health arose and the Marshal said:

I don't feel well at all. Anyone who has suffered from cerebral meningitis would be as well off if they died from it. For it either kills one or leaves one a helpless idiot. And I should know – I've had it three times.

*   *   *

What makes an Irishman envious of the French is the completedness of their culture.

*   *   *

The slums of France have a quality of cleanliness and light that you'd not find in the deserts of East London or the Gorbals, or Malpas Street for that matter.

*   *   *

My mother once said she'd like to see Paris before she died and my other respected parent muttered: 'There's not much chance of you seeing it afterwards.' But if she does want to see Paris she'd better go before she dies; it's only good Americans go there afterwards.

*   *   *

France is a great place for the Irish. You'd always feel at home there . . . and there's the same Irish excuse for getting into a political argument there.

*   *   *

I went to the Pergola bar and the proprietor let me know he remembered me from another visit a long time before. I told him I was only passing through this time and he smiled even more cordially and did not seem at all upset at the prospect of my imminent departure . . . he remembered me all right!

*   *   *

In a less civilised country there's many a French writer would have spent his life in the production of mailbags, four stitches to the inch.

*   *   *

I love France – but when I say that I don't include the cops because they are peasants and mental invalids there just as they are anywhere else.

Then as an afterthought:

Of course, the world is a madhouse and who better to patrol it than armed idiots?

*   *   *

Paris is not an expensive city and it's even cheaper when the tourist gets it into his cliggin that the laws of have it yourself or be without apply here just as they do in any other part of this sinful world.

*   *   *

The English you meet on the Continent suffer a hangover from the days when a pound was a pound and every man could wallop his own nigger.

*   *   *

His friend Dermot was often a commentator on life on the Continent.

Dermot says that he never knew a Swede who wasn't either a freak or a fraud. My own prejudice is not generally directed against the Swedish people – my granny used to say, 'It wasn't them that caused the Famine.'

*   *   *

He was asked by a Spanish reporter what event he would most enjoy attending in Spain. His reply:

Franco's funeral.

The Literary Lark

There was many 'a lark' in the Behan life. The ecclesiastical lark, the fashion lark, the pokey lark – but the literary lark was the one that mattered. The writing began in Paris, the spark of genius was fanned by the Irish Press *and then came* Borstal Boy, *and the plays, followed erratically by his 'tape-recorded books'. It was all something more now than just a lark. . . .*

*   *   *

I took up writing because it's easier than house painting.

*   *   *

In Paris I did bits of writing, mostly dirty stories, bits of house painting and one or two stints as a sailor. It was like the end of one road over the mountain and facing another one.

*   *   *

I took up writing because I like money; I envy the fella who can produce a roll of notes thick enough to choke a bull.

*   *   *

Too much money isn't good for a writer. I manage better when I'm skint.

*   *   *

I'm a journalist by accident but a creative writer by profession.

*   *   *

'*What year did you stop writing your newspaper column, Brendan?*'

How the effin' hell would I know the date? Dates is only for the police.

*   *   *

Brendan's Irish Press *column appeared on the centre pages of the paper, two pages on from the book pages. Regular contributors on the book pages included Benedict Kiely, Francis MacManus, Gabriel Fallon, Stephen Rynne and Joseph Tomelty. Once in a reference to his colleagues Brendan began:*

Round the corner there, on the more literary pages of this newspaper, it would be a reserved sin to pass any manner of a disrespectful remark about tinkers. There's great tinker-fanciers in them parts as the poem says:

> Alanna Machree, now listen to me,
> Me darlint go to res'.
> You're safe from harm, all snug and warm,
> Wrapped up in your *Irish Press*.

* * *

The only thing a writer needs is sobriety.

* * *

Proust says that to work all you need is chastity and water – neither would suit me well.

* * *

Singing your own songs or reading your own work is a form of mental incest.

* * *

A Dublin literary figure accosted Brendan. 'Well,' he said, 'how are you – hack?'

I was a hack, before you came up.

*   *   *

The key to reading *Ulysses* is to treat it like a comedian would – as a sort of gag book.

*   *   *

When Borstal Boy *was banned in Ireland (it still is) he was hurt – but he tried to laugh at it. He made up his own words to the tune of 'MacNamara's Band'.*

> Oh, me name is Brendan Behan, I'm the latest of the banned,
> Although we're small in numbers we're the best banned in the land,
> We're read at wakes and weddin's and in every parish hall,
> And under library counters sure you'll have no trouble at all.

At the end of the song he would bellow:

I've banned the Censorship Board and there's no appeal from my decision.

*   *   *

The number of people who buy books in Ireland would not keep me in drink for the duration of Sunday opening time.

* * *

Once he was arguing with:

A person who writes plays and has another occupation . . . he's an ex-officer of the law . . . a legal person in Ireland. He says to me: 'My plays will be remembered long after you are dead and rotten.' 'Well,' I said, 'I want to tell you something and that is this. First of all I'm not interested in having my plays remembered after I'm dead and rotten. Second, I don't particularly like the thought of being dead and rotten.'

* * *

'The theatre is a secret society,' said a critic. Replied Brendan:

I'm living proof that it isn't; if it was I'd still be white-washing ceilings and climbing sixty-foot ladders.

* * *

The critics couldn't make their minds up about my new play [*The Hostage*] – if it had been a murder affair I'd have suspected foul play.

* * *

I don't see why a writer should be cohesive, any more than plumbers or bankers should be cohesive.

*   *   *

Once I heard that somebody had shouted 'blasphemy' at the presentation of *The Hostage* in the Olympia, I knew I was in the tradition of O'Casey and Synge.

*   *   *

There were complaints about The Hostage *when it played in New York. Brendan stood up at a Press conference:*

Of course it's blasphemous . . . all my plays are blasphemous. But I'll invite Cardinal Spellman to see it.

*   *   *

After the successful opening of The Hostage *Brendan came back to Ireland:*

A successful dollar earner. Let's say that at the moment I don't have to worry about the price of a pound of rashers.

*   *   *

Although the Abbey turned down his play The Quare Fellow *it was still produced in this famous Dublin theatre some years after it became a world success. Challenged about letting them have it Brendan replied simply:*

It brings a few bar, doesn't it?

*   *   *

After the successful opening of The Hostage *in the West End he was asked about his political views:*

When I was in prison in England, I thought the English should clear out of Ireland and I still think so. If somebody should ask me for to clear out the Irish playwrights from the West End, then I would tell them that we are thinking of that as a reprisal.

*   *   *

He was asked to describe The Hostage *and instead he reminisced:*

It should strike you like the old pantomimes at the Queen's – fun laced with vulgarity.

*   *   *

John B Keane was going to give a reading of his poems at Alphonsus Sweeney's pub and he took Brendan along with him.

Brendan advised me to stop feckin' about with poetry and

write dramas about the people I knew. 'Poetry is all right,' said Brendan, 'but it's all written.'

* * *

You wouldn't want to be minding them poet fellows, they're a dangerous clique be the best of times.

* * *

In 1957 he was talking to Kenneth Allsop, then writing for the Daily Mail, *about his own beginnings as a writer.*

Ten years ago in Strangeways Prison I stopped trying to find political solutions and began being a writer.

* * *

Brendan grabbed Kenneth Allsop's arm after the Dublin interview and pointed:

There you are, didn't I tell you I was a proletarian writer? Dublin will never forget my work.

In front of them on a hotel wall were tall black letters, the output of an earlier period. 'No Parking', they said. . . .

* * *

At a Yorkshire Post *luncheon where there were many children present, Brendan, forewarned by his friend Val Iremonger, spoke for nearly an hour without once using any words to which anyone could object. But later when he had finished his speech he could not contain himself any longer. As a well-known editor of a literary magazine passed across the room, he whispered to his companion:*

Look at that professional Jesus!

*   *   *

Brendan savagely denied to Derek Hart, in a BBC interview, that his success had been of any benefit to him.

I go to better beds, if you like, but I sleep less well.

*   *   *

In America they teach journalism, but in France it just overtakes you.

*   *   *

In New York:

Whenever you want me to go on television you only have to say the word. Money.

*   *   *

New York newspapers go on for ever about nothing.

*   *   *

Joyce was something of a natural phenomenon. . . .
Maybe there were two eggs and mine hatched later than his.

*   *   *

If people are willing to pay nearly £1 for a book of mine
it shows that they're not merely buying it because they heard
I was drunk on television, or that I sang a song for the buskers
outside the Wyndham's Theatre in the West End of London
while my own show was going on. I thought it a perfectly
natural thing to do. I've been a busker myself . . . not a very
successful one.

*   *   *

*He criticised the book by the Irish writer St John Ervine on
Carson, 'that Dublin-Italian', by saying that:*

Mr Irvine hates us, the Irish, because we're Eireanns.
Every damned one of us – Oscar Wilde, the 'Bird' Flanagan,
Father O'Flynn, Bishop Berkeley, the Colleen Bawn, Mat
the Thrasher, Burke and Hare, the Rakes of Mallow, the
Boys of Wexford, and Bernard Shaw – gets off with a
caution for having been born in Dolphin's Barn.

*   *   *

Talking about his unfinished play Richard's Cork Leg *he said:*

I told a steward on the boat a joke from the play and he laughed . . . and if it'll make a steward on the Cunard Line laugh it'll rock Broadway.

*   *   *

Commenting later on Richard's Cork Leg *he said that it was about sex, religion and politics because:*

Nothing else is worth considering anyway.

*   *   *

Commenting on a reported statement by Joan Littlewood that his play Richard's Cork Leg *was 'so Rabelaisian in its bawdyness and Swiftian in its satire that she is not sure how she will produce it', Brendan said that he had great confidence in her judgment.*

As a matter of fact she has accused me of writing Catholic propaganda under the guise of anti-clericalism.

*   *   *

Brendan and Beatrice were frequent theatregoers in the late fifties. If you met him at Dublin's Gate Theatre you were likely to be greeted with:

This is my missus, and this is Lord Longford and his missus.

*　　　*　　　*

'What was the message of your play, Mr Behan?' asked a reporter. Bellowed the playwright:

Message? What do you think I am . . . a bloody telegram boy?

*　　　*　　　*

Brendan once described John Osborne as being:

As effin' angry as Mrs Dale.

*　　　*　　　*

'What do you think of Joyce?' asked a reporter.

They shouldn't have hanged him.

*　　　*　　　*

Brendan once reviewed a Dublin try-out of a West End play and commented:

It's impact was like the banging together of two damp dish-cloths.

The Dying Lark

'*Dying as a lark*,' said Brendan, '*has no attraction for me.*' It was another of those lonely businesses and not one he was looking forward to. But while he could he mocked death and he was always one to bury the dead with sympathy plus cheerfulness, which, as Benedict Kiely wrote, mocked at mortality. Even his own funeral on a dreary March day in 1964 would have given him a smile. A speaker at the graveside said he'd had the privilege of being 'interred' with Brendan. Interned, he meant; and while Brendan had his reservations about internment during his life he surely would have preferred it to the permanency of the plot in Glasnevin.

*　　　*　　　*

There's no bad publicity except an obituary.

*　　　*　　　*

After the film The Quare Fella *Brendan told Eamonn Andrews:*

I don't like the dying lark at all. I don't think anyone does. I can give you instances of very eminent men surrounding themselves with all kinds of quacks, all sorts of doctors and surgeons and scientists, in an attempt to stop in this world just a little while longer. A fellow said we know where we are; we're not quite sure where we're going.

Eamonn: Well, none of us is quite sure where he's going, but wherever . . .

Brendan: You are. You're quite sure you're not going to die. Anyone that appears on television so often as you do is under the opinion that they're going to live to be about a hundred and fifty. And then you'll have one of these things [a camera] over you to get your last minutes.

*   *   *

The best words any man can ever hear at his funeral:

Carry on with the coffin . . . the corpse'll walk.

*   *   *

After once leaving hospital against doctor's advice he said:

I'm only staying alive to save funeral expenses.

*   *   *

The poor have the cheek and the impudence to die on nothing and they get married on even less.

* * *

Playwright Seamus Byrne knew Brendan well and was very fond of him:

I remember one of the last times I met him. I hadn't seen him for quite a while and he'd changed beyond all recognition. I said: 'Brendan, how are you?' and he answered, 'If they tell us what's true, we're all dying, so why should I complain?'

* * *

Remembers ballad writer Jimmy Hiney:

One day, a few years ago, I went to the funeral of Lord Longford at Mount Jerome outside Dublin. And there with the hundreds of mourners was Brendan. Dressed in his best he was, fine suit, black tie and all. He sees me and comes up to me, no doubt wondering if we should go into the Protestant church or not. Or anyway wondering if I would go in. He looked down at me and one of his curly locks fell over his eyes. 'Jimmy,' says he, putting a large arm around my shoulders, 'Jimmy, I think we'll go in and sing a few hymns for the oul' bugger. He has as much chance of heaven as either of us.'

*   *   *

At heart I am a daylight atheist but I would not like to die without a priest.

*   *   *

Alan Brien, then theatre critic of the Daily Telegraph, *asked Brendan if he ever thought about death.*

Think about it? I'd rather be dead than think about it.

*   *   *

Karate-type humour wasn't unknown to Brendan. Once he met a former friend in a pub and said:

I hear there's someone dead belonging to you – it's not yourself by any chance?

*   *   *

When I die I want to die in bed surrounded by fourteen holy nuns with candles. I am a Catholic, a damn bad one according to some. Even when the drink takes to me I find that when darkness falls I think of my prayers.

*   *   *

As Brendan lay dying on 20th March 1964, apparently in a coma, an attentive nun hovered about solicitously. As she bent over him a last time to smooth a pillow, Brendan opened one dark eye and whispered to her:

Thank you, Sister – may you be the mother of a bishop!